A View Into the Mind of Asperger's
Book 2 - Waiting for Trains

A View Into the Mind of Asperger's
Book 2 - Waiting for Trains

S. Lea

I Street Press

© Copyright April 2021, S. Lea

All rights reserved. No portion of this book may be reproduced, stored in a retrieval system, or transmitted in any form by any means – electronic, mechanical, photocopying, recording or otherwise –without prior permission of the copyright owner.

Lea, S
A View Into the Mind of Asperger's
Book 2 - Waiting for Trains by S. Lea

ISBN: 978-163795662-5

Library of Congress Control Number: 2021901131

Cover Design by Website Imagine

Illustrations by Janet L. Rau
Edited by: Janey Ranlett
Continuity Consultant – j EG
Technical Advisor – J.A.C.

FIRST EDITION

Printed in the United States of America

I Street Press
828 I Street
Sacramento, CA   95814

Dad

You'll be Happy to Know…..

This book is dedicated to all the Teachers and Specialists who supported us.

Preface

Second in a series of Train books, 'Waiting for Trains' is as an attempt to provide what I never had almost two decades ago, when my son was diagnosed with what was then called a 'Verbal Learning Disability'. Over the years this condition has became part of the Autistic Spectrum, and is now more commonly called Asperger's.

All those years ago there was very little information on the condition, and even less on facing its challenges. There were no suggestions for parents on how to improve day to day life for these children, their siblings or their extended family.

Readers of the first book, 'Chasing Trains', will notice some of the same material is covered in 'Waiting for Trains'. I could not assume readers would be familiar with the first book so I felt it necessary to include certain important information.

As the school system faced challenges on how best to assist in the education of an Asperger's child, I faced the challenges of day to day life.

Books and other reference material of the time contained, for the most part, descriptions of behaviors and depictions of "symptoms" associated with Asperger's.

Symptoms his teachers and I were painfully aware of. There was very little information on how we could improve his day to day life and nothing that even resembled advice.

In Waiting for Trains I focus on balancing home life with school life in the early years. Continuing to use his passion for trains as a tool, through trial and error I discovered ways to make his daily life at school, and in the public arena, more positive and rewarding.

As my son moved through elementary school and middle school, thankfully, the education system became more aware of the needs of this distinct population. The increased awareness validated that my son's challenges were not all about my parenting style, as some suspected. This was a real issue being faced by parents and being faced by the school system.

By partnering with teachers, specialists, and the school system at large, I was able to help my son get the most out of the time he spent in that world. However, when the lights went out and the classroom door was locked for the day, I was still on my own.

This book describes techniques I used to balance school life and home life, by embracing my son's passion for trains to help him succeed in both worlds.

I hope 'Waiting for Trains' will give parents the courage to seek out solutions, and do what they know in their hearts is right. More importantly I hope parents reading this book will toss out what makes no sense to them, and try the things that do.

Contents

Preface		i
Introduction		1
Chapter 1	The "Eyes" Have It	11
Chapter 2	What's Old Is New Again	23
Chapter 3	You Have to Search From Your Heart to Find Angels	37
Chapter 4	Self 'E-Steam'	47
Chapter 5	"Bully for You"	55
Chapter 6	"Tattling the Truth"	63
Chapter 7	R-E-S-P-E-C-T	71
Chapter 8	Rubik's Cube Parenting	83
Chapter 9	The Safety Net	93
Chapter 10	Staying Off the 'Pity-Pot'	107
Chapter 11	Those 'Other' Days…..	119
Chapter 12	"ALL ABOARD "	125

Introduction

This book, second in a series, is intended to share information with other parents of children diagnosed with Asperger's. Information that was not available to me all those years ago when a diagnosis of Asperger's was actually quite rare. Information that I hope will assist in helping to make day to day challenges a little less taxing.

Like the first book, this is not meant to be a sad sob tale of the difficulties and stresses relating to raising a child with Asperger's, but you may possibly experience emotional moments, as you relate to what I describe.

There are many who believe, as I do, that if your child does not have a focused passion for a single subject, then the diagnosis of Asperger's may not be altogether correct. This is not science, just a belief.

This book presumes you suspect a diagnosis of Asperger's, or already have one. It pre-supposes that your child has difficulty with communication and that you may face melt-downs that seem to come from nowhere.

To my thinking, crying is a passive act, one I've indulged in. Writing, talking, sharing is 'action' and feels so much better overall. I hope you can put some of the suggestions into 'action' and I hope they work for you as well.

The purpose of this book is not to identify a "cure". Making your child "act" like a typical child is not the goal. The purpose is to share techniques that helped me maneuver through day to day life with a child diagnosed with Asperger's.

This book will continue to acknowledge that, just like with any typical child, different things work for different children. It is meant to bring you, as a parent of an Asperger's child, some real life suggestions based on discoveries; and believe me, quite by accident most times, that worked to help my son and I live a daily life which was much less stressful.

These suggestions are just that, suggestions. They may not work for you and your family, but hopefully, they will bring you to a place that makes you comfortable with trying anything new, anything different that helps.

It doesn't matter why something works or doesn't work. I'm asking that you keep trying new things until you find success. Success, for the purpose of this book, is being in a place where day to day life is less stressful, more enjoyable, and frees you of some of eggshells you walk on each day.

Why you and your child happened upon this situation is not the focus of this book. That question must be dealt with, and answered, by the professionals, the geneticists, and of course, the 'almighty' pharmaceutical industry giants.

I am not a researcher, a scientist, a child psychologist, or a child development expert, but I am a well educated individual, with the added value of 'experience' with an Asperger's child 24/7 for over 20 years.

While I may not be revered by everyone in the 'professional' community, given my resume, I feel confident that you may find some value, in some form, by reading this book. Whether you find practical knowledge, things you are willing to try, or whether it is more abstract ideas you have pondered yourself I hope you can gain from this book.

While dealing with all the time consuming tasks of day to day life my first priority was raising my son. With lots of energy and commitment I knew the importance of making him the focus, yet still needed time to deal with life 'maintenance' of things like 'money' (job), cleanliness (laundry and house), reliable transportation (cars), shopping (food), and don't forget the pets...

Like any child, if my son was entertained for bits of time I could get to other necessary tasks. I had a strategy with toys and his passion for trains which thankfully gave me bits of time to get everything done. It also gave him time to explore new things. Check out the Toy chapter, you may find it helpful.

The chapters about teachers and the school system disclose that I am a huge fan. Whether you are willing to accept it or not.....though you have that very, very, "special little individual" you call your child... teachers have the exceptional experience of dealing with hundreds of parent's "special little individuals".

As the number of children diagnosed with Asperger's unfortunately continues to grow, the teachers familiar with Asperger's and have some expertise, is fortunately growing in numbers as well.

I've always spent a lot of my energy making sure that the son I've been given is prized and loved and given every opportunity to thrive. Part of that thriving would absolutely depend on, not only how I deal with him, but also how I deal with family, teachers, and the public.

My original thought about writing this series was to outline time frames and milestones in age progression. What I have found, is that with each particular issue, its first appearance might be at one age, but the same issue would resurface in a slightly different form at a later age. Techniques for handling the same issue changed based on what was age appropriate at the time.

In the early years I, of course, dealt with the basics like eating, sleeping, dressing, child care and the like. In later years some of those same issues would re-appear in a slightly different form. I had to make adjustments to my techniques depending on when and where the issues arose.

Communication issues were paramount in the early years. Trying to form a meaningful connection through words was a huge concern. Developing the ability to use language as a tool to get through a tough situation was a major focus early on.

Later, even though we would talk more frequently, the issue of communication re-appears in a different form. In those later years, as my son's world expanded, the information that should have been communicated was just as difficult to get to, as in the early years.

I will describe our travels and how people were astounded at a nine year olds knowledge and expertise about trains, both the workings and the history. Yet, in later years people might look at that same knowledge and his communication style as being almost 'rude'.

Absolutely without question the safety issues I dealt with in the early years, when he was under constant care and supervision, were vastly different than the safety issues as he grew, was more independent, and was not always in earshot or view.

As my son moved on in age there were things I had overlooked at an earlier age for various reasons. Things that many kids learn by observation I had essentially forgotten to teach him even though they were basic life skills.

Velcro is great, but what about tying shoes. Microwaves are great, but what about the safety of the oven and the stovetop. I was so used to taking care of everything I had forgotten he needed to learn these things for himself.

Interestingly, as he did start communicating more in some ways, it could often be even more difficult to keep things calm and sane as I often got only partial information. This could be almost more frustrating than when he hardly communicated at all. When it came to his day at school it was difficult if not impossible for me to discern the goings on of his day. I was always concerned that I was missing out on important information.

This is where the teachers and education system helped me fill in the gaps. Partnering with teachers is by far one of the most important things I did for my son. I felt if my son was to learn and grow, I would need to be knowledgeable and support his life at school. After all, that's where he spent half his waking hours.

This began our journey into meeting some of the smartest, most convivial folks I would ever meet. It helped me not only support his education, but helped teachers to better support my son. As I see it, there is no down side here.

One of the paramount issues for parents, not only of Asperger's kids, but in the general population, is the fight against "bullying". Somehow that act of a bully puts us in a place of deep sorrow, while at the same time, makes us feel the same sense of anger and aggression they apply. It's hard to feel sorry for a bully, but they are likely dealing with some tough issues of their own.

Thankfully, Asperger's in my son provided an almost invisible shield towards those bullies. Being unaware of the social nuances of behavior, if someone was bullying him his lack of concern and recognition protected him from it. Bullying is effective for socially concerned individuals. Where Asperger's lacks social graces and understanding at times, this can almost serve as a protection from feeling bad since the actions of a bully might not even register. "There is a God !"

What you will not see in this book are descriptions of the times that were unmanageable. This is by design. I don't find it useful to re-hash all the difficulties, the 'errors' if you will, as it serves no purpose. I'm sure you've had enough difficulties of your own. Commiserating, although good for the soul, doesn't always result in changes that move us forward.

Don't think for one moment that I just breezed through and came up with all these great ideas that helped my son succeed. On the contrary, for every discovery, and every 'win', there were multiple defeats.

I just want parents to have something I did not have all those years ago. Information not only on 'symptoms' that you are already well-versed in, but some sort of hope that there are possible solutions.

If you take away anything from this book I hope it is two things. First, if they have a passion for a single thing, then embrace it. Use it as a tool to teach other important things in life. The time for being well rounded will come as these children experience the world. Second, if something isn't working try something different. Keep experimenting, and keep trying, until you find a solution that works for you and your child.

Chapter 1

The "Eyes" Have It

Regardless of language, culture or upbringing there are basic human traits we rely on when communicating with other individuals. It is not just the spoken word that tells us what someone is saying, it is the body language, the gestures, the facial expressions, that put communication in proper context.

If we are speaking to someone who is not looking towards us, not looking in our eyes, we wonder whether they are actually hearing us. How many times have you questioned someone, asking "are you listening to me?, simply because they are not looking directly at you as you speak.

When we speak, eye contact is most often how we determine if someone is listening 'or not'. Determining whether they are hearing us is based on whether they are looking directly at us, or at very least looking in our direction.

One of the most distinct characteristics of Asperger's is the varying degrees, and in some instances, total lack of, eye contact, when they are speaking to you. It may also include their lack of eye contact when you are speaking to them as well. This characteristic, above all, seems to alert us that something is unique and unusual about these individuals. It's what people, above all, seem to notice "is different".

In his early years my son's lack of eye contact and lack of communication seemed to go hand in hand. I was much more concerned with his lack of speech and didn't concern myself with the eye contact issue at that time. I was willing to take first things first.

As we had a somewhat one-sided relationship when it came to talking, I continued to talk to him whether I felt he was listening or not. I continued to sit and read to him whether it appeared he was grasping the story or not. I would now describe this as the single most important foundation laid for much of what would come.

That little computer chip in his brain was absorbing everything. Even though he didn't respond with words, or look at me when I spoke, the information was in fact populating his brain cells.

In the past I had recognized that when it came to my son's 'senses', as in sight, hearing, touch, taste, but not so much smell, he had a heightened level of sensitivity.

He could hear a train from miles away, here the neighbors barking dog, hear the television or maybe song on the radio, all at the same time. Can you imagine? Processing so much at one time was difficult and it would take time for him to start filtering things like most of us do naturally.

In that same vein I applied my knowledge of this phenomenon of simultaneous sensory input to what might be occurring when I spoke to him. He may well have wanted to pay attention, but so many other things were going on, it was a struggle for him.

That "something" going on when I was talking was, I believe, his attempt to focus only on my voice, on the spoken word. His lack of eye contact was an attempt to filter intentionally, as most of us would do naturally.

He needed to turn off visual contact and the distracting signals of my body language, in order to really 'hear' what I was saying. Things like eye contact, gestures, and tone were a distraction to him.

If he looked at me and had to process what he was "seeing" against a back drop of what I was saying, his eye contact could actually diminish his ability to hear me and understand me. In the same way, if he was speaking, and wanted to focus on what he was saying, it was easier if he could "turn off" distracting visual ques. This was truly a big time 'AH..HA' moment.

Then the work began. I think I may have realized the 'why' of minimal eye contact, but I knew he had to get on in this world. This world full of highly socialized human beings that expect the simple courtesy of being acknowledged by eye contact, when they are speaking. I would have to help him balance his listening, alongside being comfortable with eye contact.

Demanding that he look at me was not the route. Asking him if he was listening would never make sense to him. The more you asked him to look at you, the more heightened the distraction became. After all, if he really wanted to hear you he couldn't possibly look at you.

This was not a time for demands. This was not a time to say "please look at me". Being stern about forcing him to look at me when I spoke would most assuredly have had exactly the opposite effect. It would have created stress that could well have exacerbated the problem.

This was one of those occasions when I took the "behaviorist" approach. I would have to slowly and methodically 'teach' eye contact in a manner that was not intimidating, nor divisive. It would be taught in a way that would result in him welcoming the gesture as he might receive pleasure, a 'reward', in knowing when someone made eye contact with him, they were listening to him as well.

His special education teacher Lisa, and I, seemed to come to this same conclusion simultaneously. It would be paramount that he not just go through the motions of eye contact, but would actually welcome it. It could become second nature and part of his connection to others.

We both seemed to be using the same approach. When speaking to him, it was best to get as close in proximity as reasonable and as you spoke just "gently"…"oh so gently" apply a bit of pressure to his lower jaw, moving his eyes to align with yours.

The eye contact was subtle, non-descript, and not talked about. It was training him to hear what was being said while getting comfortable and practiced at looking towards me.

At first, I would intentionally just align his face and mine, using this soft movement, and avoid eye contact. Next, I slowly introduced what I considered a downward look, not distracting him. The next step was to keep talking while maintaining short spurts of direct eye contact. The final step was talking while directly maintaining eye contact, until the conversation was complete.

This sounds a whole lot easier than it was. It was a slow and arduous process that happened over a period of time. The result was astonishing. He, like other humans, enjoyed the connection of eye contact as a way of assuring he was also heard when he spoke.

My mom was often ahead of the game. She told me that she actually never noticed whether he was, or wasn't, looking at her when she spoke. Neither did she notice whether he was looking at her, when he spoke. Ah, the wonder of grandmas!

She was also at that time slowly, methodically, teaching him about eye contact, talking, and feeling safe. He naturally engaged with no effort at all. Not a plan, just second nature for her.

The accomplishment was not that he learned a behavior to make him appear more typical. The accomplishment was that he could enjoy a connection with other people that many of us take for granted when we talk and see each other "eye to eye."

The irony of this stigma.....since the invention of the telephone, humans have learned to adapt to two way conversations with only their voice and absolutely no eye contact or body language at all ! The bigger irony.....is with cell phones, we have managed to eliminate voice as well, mostly relying on texting.

I sometimes notice entire families at a restaurant, all on their individual cell phones seemingly not communicating with 'each other'. I wonder why they bothered to get together to engage in some family time if they seem so 'disengaged'.

What I hear is, rather than talking, these families might actually be texting each other. I also hear that entire groups of people in close proximity are not conversing but are in fact communicating via text.

I wonder, had my son had the opportunity to text others, not be expected to speak or have eye contact, would he have been singled out back then as socially different ? It's something I have pondered.

One of the best examples of our current addiction to the use of cell phones and texting was a story shared by a colleague of mine. He owned a small business and was in the market for a receptionist. He wasn't in need of a 'brain surgeon', just someone with a high school diploma and good communication skills.

Apparently he had an applicant who looked promising. Once she showed up and went through the interview process he was sure she would be a good match for the job. She was pleasant, gregarious, and seemed very motivated.

He was convinced she was a good fit for the job and needed her to perform one last task, clear one last hurdle, to secure a job offer. He gave her a brief overview of the phone system (answering, putting calls on hold, and ringing another line). He then informed her he would step into another room and "ring her". She would need to answer the phone and greet him as she would a customer. She would need to ask a series of questions, all based on the written script he had provided.

He left the room and continued to his office. He allowed a fair amount of time for her to review the 'script'. He then proceeded to dial the business line. The phone rang...no answer. He tried once again, making sure he was calling the line from the 'outside'. The phone rang and rang...and again, no answer.

As he re-entered the room he discovered this possible new hire was nowhere to be found. The phone sat quietly on the table with no one in attendance should it ring.

As he proceeded to look for his 'interviewee', he walked down the hallway and out towards the front of the building. He then heard the distinct sound of what he described as "flying gravel and screeching tires". He also caught a brief glimpse of the back of the RAM truck she had borrowed from her folks to get to the interview.

As he shared this story with me the next day, we concluded that the poor little thing hadn't been exposed to a land line since she was likely a small child. A time when her parents had forced her to say a few words to grandma on the weekly Sunday call. She was so unfamiliar with a land line, so terrified to speak on a phone, rather than text, she did the only thing a truly 'panicked' person does….. Run like hell!

Despite our use of cell phones and texting, when we have "live" and up-close communication, we still use eye contact as the gold standard. My son would be held to this standard, so it was important for me to help him meet this challenge.

I knew hands down when the goal of having eye contact, in unison with having a conversation, was achieved. As he spoke to me one day about what I am sure was a very important tidbit on train history, he commented, I was apparently "not listening". How did he discern I was not listening? I of course, was not looking at him.

Suggestion

If you are experiencing a lack of eye contact, take it slow and easy, but do take it on. This will be of the utmost importance for the rest of your child's life. (cell phones, or not)

Chapter 2

What's Old Is New Again

My son's passion for trains made supplying entertainment and toys exceptionally easy. Trains are, and have been, a standard in the toy industry for years and years. There were train sets, train books, train videos, and don't forget, this was the beginning of the "Thomas Era".

Wooden trains, plastic trains motorized and remote trains. Not to mention the old fashioned "build it yourself" train layouts. The possibilities, when it comes to trains, are endless.

When I had the funds I added to his toy and media inventory. When family members purchased birthday and Christmas gifts it was always an easy decision. One could never have enough of trains when it came to my son.

Occasionally someone would venture out and wrap up a tractor or a car. I never had to be embarrassed at 'his' response. It would be the rest of the family who would turn towards that person with a look that essentially said, "Really?" "Are you out of your mind?"

Did I indulge my son? Absolutely I did. Did it result in a need for more and more of the "right" toys, the "right" engines? Well, sometimes. But it was more my doing. I wanted to make sure he had enough to keep him busy when I needed time for cooking, cleaning, or paying bills.

With no siblings, it was up to me to keep him occupied. I had to make sure he was not only occupied, but busy doing something within my earshot and eyesight, as there was no one else around to report possible issues.

For those parents with multiple children you probably, at times, enjoy a bit of a break when they keep each other occupied. At the same time, with the various disputes and issues that come up between siblings may make it even more challenging to keep things in check when all you need is a precious few minutes.

With two parents in the household maybe one can watch over the kids, while the other takes care of business? But I have no frame of reference to determine if that works.

What I can say, is that I had to live in the only world I knew, and that world is the world I write about. I'm sure you have different challenges, so I urge you to write a book of your own. It may help families with similar challenges as yours.

My son is bright and became easily bored if new things were not introduced. He wasn't the type of kid that would get the same pleasure out of single toy or a single train running endlessly, around the same track. He tired easily of anything that was "pre-determined" by design.

Like most folks, I don't have an unlimited supply of money to constantly purchase new things. If I could spend a bit of money, I was very careful about what I chose as toys. I wanted to assure that the toys and books I bought had the "depth" necessary to keep my son's interest as he changed and matured.

I equally relied on basics like construction paper, crayons, cotton balls, glue, and anything I could find at the 'dollar store'. These things were also important because they required my time and my involvement when building great train 'things.'

Being a self-admitted obsessive-compulsive individual, I always had to make sure everything not only had a place, but landed in that place by the end of each the day. Because that is my nature, it wasn't until I looked back, that I realized it had a very positive effect on my son.

I made sure he had toys and books and things accessible while I was doing the daily chores. It was also my practice that no matter how many toys and trains were pulled out during the evening, it was absolutely essential, that everything be put away at the end of play time.

When he was very young we had the "pre-fab" already designed versions of train tracks. I would put them together, with him watching every move, and once it was done, "voila" he could press the button and the train would move along nicely on a set course.

I would then rush in to make dinner or write up bills, or just sit on the patio with a glass of wine, pondering the next day. Time passed, bath time approached, and I would pick up the train tracks for safe keeping for the next day.

Once everything was picked up he knew it was bath time. He knew it was time to settle in on the one-on-one time we had while he was in the tub. I urged him to help with the clean up but, as is my nature, I would hurriedly just get it done myself. For a period of time, not quite sure how long, this was our routine.

One evening, dinner dishes put away and not quite ready to clear the train layout, I sat for a time. I was not ready for bath time, but he clearly was. He came to me fussing, not at all interested in his train. I picked up the toys as usual, and we went on to bath time.

The next day it was the same thing. He had clearly grown bored with watching the train go round and round and round. It was great that he waited for the clean-up, and did not seem to be bothered until it was done, but I had a sense that this was again a time when alterations to our daily routine were in order.

Something had changed. The same ol', same ol' was no longer working. These are the cues that you need to hone in on. Asperger's kids are best when things are as predictable as possible, but when predictability isn't working, it's best that you look at it as 'progress', and move on to a new routine.

At that time, "Thomas the Train" was all the rage. There were TV shows, videos, train engines and train tracks. I began purchasing these items, as did the family. My son seemed to develop an even keener interest in trains.

Wooden tracks that were straight, wooden tracks that were curved, all became a part of his collection. There were bridges, viaducts, crossings and numerous train engines, all with names.

If you watched the videos, each of these engines had distinct personalities. Each story conveyed a set of ideas like helpfulness, boasting, taking care of others and many other lessons of life.

As the wooden track inventory grew, he began building his own layouts, his own expanded designs. One day it would be a round track, next day a figure eight, next day, a long expanse with just a tunnel near the end.

With the engines and cars, vehicles and buses and sometimes helicopters, the sequencing, or what we refer to as the 'Con'sist (pronounced like 'con'vict) in train lingo, varied on a daily basis.

Funny thing is, when he first started telling me about the 'con'sist of a train I always corrected him, explaining that it was pronounced consist'. I just assumed at his early age, when he read the word, he was pronouncing it wrong. Shame on me, I should have known better.

At one of our outings with other train folks I overheard my son and a man talking about the 'con'sist. I now realized that is how train people refer to the make-up and sequence of the cars. When it came to train information I began to acknowledge that he was accurate, not most of the time, but all of the time.

Even with this renewed interest and increased engagement I continued to insist that at the end of the evening, just before bath time, all would be put away, and in its designated place. I purchased several blue plastic bins which would serve as storage for these new, "oh so important" discoveries.

Every piece of track was dismantled and randomly put into a blue bin and stored away each night. The next day at playtime he would pull out the bins and empty them onto the family room floor which was large enough to accommodate most any layout he could possibly imagine.

Each day was like a 'new discovery' for him, a new day in designing a track layout. Maybe he came upon the crossing first, or the long track versus short track. He could use his brain to put something together that was novel and very different from the day before.

Thomas could be pulling the train on a Tuesday, but by Wednesday it might be James, and by Thursday maybe Gordon. The 'con'sist might include the 'Troublesome Trucks" or maybe not. He was enjoying play time again. Each day could be a new design, a new story.

I continued to build the track inventory and we still have every single piece. I hope someday he can pass them along to another young train enthusiast. This collection represents hours and hours of play, which encouraged new thoughts each time a layout was built.

What I learned was that by putting these toys away each day, allowing the next day to be a new choice of what is going to be used, helped to exercise his brain and his imagination. Not to mention, the "boredom" was all but eliminated.

We were back to playtime leading into bath time on a set schedule. I also became more patient and insisted he help to put everything away, even though it took a bit longer than before.

As the years went by, even at an older age, when his older cousins were visiting, those tracks and those engines would be pulled out and a new track plan would be discovered and enjoyed.

Toys are that, just toys. They are meant to entertain, and if chosen carefully, they can also teach. If they are just strewn about and left day after day they can become quite mundane to a child. They become part of the decorum of the house just like the chair, or the rug, or the kitchen table…"BOORRR…ING…!"

Not to mention…. how many of you have awoken during the night, made your way to the kitchen for a drink of water, and stepped on the proverbial sharp, plastic toy? Doesn't that feel great?

You can have a 20 by 20-foot room and one tiny little 2 by 2- inch Lego piece, but by God, your foot will land squarely on that tiny little piece, every time. It's some kind of universal law, like butter side down.

Not only will it land on this tiny sharp object, it will never be on the surface of your hard, protected heel. It will always be in your most vulnerable spot, the soft spot where your toe and foot are connected. This allows for the maximum allowable pain.

The event is usually accompanied by a loud yell, and often a series of expletives, oh….##!!**. The pain is excruciating but dissipates quickly. If anyone else has the good fortune to be in earshot, or actually be a witness, it's hilarious! Hilarious for them of course…. not so hilarious for you.

If for no other reason, try to put everything away before bedtime so you won't have to deal with an obstacle course through the night.

When toys are tucked away, and newly discovered at a future date, they become more entertaining and valuable again.

Likewise, when I would get out the construction paper, crayons, glue and the like, usually on a rainy Saturday or Sunday, my son and I would put together a paper layout. The layout would then be displayed on his bedroom wall.

We would start with the engine, move to the tender, whether coal or wood, and then move on to coaches, baggage cars and the best was when we did Circus Trains!

We often left them posted to the wall for a week, maybe two. However, at some point we pulled it down, tucked it away and look forward to another rainy day to put together something even better than the one before.

I'm not suggesting that when you put away toys, or artwork, or projects that they necessarily be sight unseen. They just have to have a "place". Based on space and numbers of kids, or toys, bookcases purchased at a garage sale, stackable bins, or as in my case blue plastic bins, work quite nicely.

On those days when you are absolutely wiped out and picking up toys seems as hard as climbing Mt. Everest, I propose this plan……have the kid(s) pick up the toys. How does that sound?

In addition to toys, books were a constant in our household. Whether it was after dinner, or just before bedtime, I would pull out a book, and take a load off my feet while I read to him. And in many cases, he would read to me.

During those "Thomas" years I was able to purchase the book "Thomas the Tank Engine, The Complete Collection" written by Reverend Wilbert Awdry. After that, I also purchased "The New Collection" written by his son, Christopher Awdry.

At that time there was no Amazon. No E-Bay, where you could purchase gently used books at a discount. So, I would save up and pay full price. Full price actually became "priceless" in terms of his reading skills and his understanding of the relationships and emotions of these train personalities.

His exposure to life lessons described through the characters, not to mention the extraordinary vocabulary presented, was surely worth the investment. His love of all things 'trains' made it easy for him to read the stories presented in the books.

These stories helped him to understand the world. The world as it unfolds through relationships. In this case, the relationships of many little locomotives and cars with distinct personalities. These little trains could use their attributes for good cause, but also, occasionally, fall prey, to their faults.

These books would teach him to use vocabulary in the proper context. Although he was an infrequent communicator, when he did communicate, the words just rolled-out in a syntax and style that was quite extraordinary. This I attribute to the vast amount of reading he did on his own, and we did together.

I made sure to have him read aloud to me often. This would assure me he was pronouncing properly, and understanding the content of the story.

I added books to my son's collection as finances allowed. Again, there were, and still are, so many possibilities when it comes to train related books.

Whatever it is your child has a passion for, seek out resource material and books on the subject. As they read and absorb the content, make sure to be an active participant in the process. There's a lot to be learned in unlikely places.

Don't try to time the books to your child's current level. Get something a bit above that level and let them "give it a go".

Suggestion:

Tuck the toys away at the end of the day. This may lead to "new" discoveries in the future.
(Not to mention, save your toes)

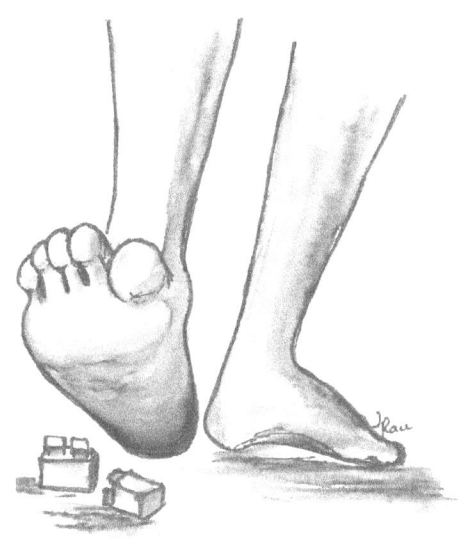

Chapter 3

You Have to Search From Your Heart to Find Angels

I believe that everyone might well have an angel watching over them. The only way to find that angel is through your heart. You may see them right in front of you and not know this is your angel. It is only when you open your heart and 'look back' that you discover the truth.

My son and I shared the same angel and we thankfully met our angel very early on. This angel's earthly name is Lisa. She came to us in the form of a special education teacher at his elementary school.

Lisa is the kind of person who enters a room and brings with her an energy level that is palpable. Her hair has a shimmer which makes it hard to describe exactly what color it is. A mix of golden with lighter highlights, a thickness which is rich, but moves about, as easily, as she moves about.

Her eyes are striking but project the warmth she possesses. She is not of daunting height but neither is she a tiny little thing. She is 'just right'.

Her smile is contagious and when she asks "How are you?" it is not just a courtesy, she really wants to know.

Her kindness and commitment to "her kids," is self-evident. She is one of those rare birds who doesn't just talk about how everyone is an individual, but embodies that concept in how she goes about her work.

Along with her warmth and commitment she possesses a fierce drive to fight as needed for her cause. She may come into a room with positive energy determined to present her case, but unless you have nothing but good intentions, you better stand by, as she'll see right through you, and 'call you out'.

As part of staying engaged in my son's daily 'goings on' at school I set up a meeting with his special education teacher. This is when I met Lisa who had already spent time with my son and was surely on her way to what I thought would be a 'plan'.

When I entered the room she approached as if holding back a hug she surely wanted to extend, but simply introduced herself. Our meeting was in her work area and we sat in the "little chairs".

This was the first time I experienced her eyes, so radiant, as she held her tears to a manageable level, never letting them flow down a cheek. This was when I first saw her beautiful smile but noticed it was slightly turned down to one side, as she struggled to keep the quiver of her chin in check. This is when I knew, "holy shit", there is no plan.

At that moment I knew her mind had been challenged to reach out and understand my son and find every resource available to help him. This was when, I absolutely knew, that her heart had been irrevocably changed.

So Lisa and I, and of course my son, became the first of first's at this elementary school, and began our trek off into the unknown world of dealing with Asperger's.

She used her expertise to try to help my son be successful in school but also took on a very similar approach to what I was doing at home. She would try things, but if they didn't work, she would try something else. She absolutely embraced his love of trains and found a way to capture his attention using trains as a method to teach something else.

One of my most vivid memories is a day I arrived early to pick up my son and decided to go see Lisa, say hello, and catch up on progress. When I walked into her room I needed to check the time to assure I would be outside my son's classroom when he got out for the day. Low and behold, there it was. A little train, obviously fashioned by a grade school student, with the signature cut out and coloring style of my son. It was placed high up on the classroom clock and I knew immediately she was using this train to help him learn to tell time.

Imagine my competing emotions. I was so touched that 'my' chin was now the one that had to be kept in check....yet it was also so funny I couldn't help but smile. When she looked at my reaction, we both laughed. We laughed together as if we had just heard the funniest joke ever told.

As part of their lack of social graces, when one reaches out to hug an Asperger's kid, they most often do not respond in-kind, and almost never hug back. I believe, Lisa being a very warm, 'hugging' type of person, took this on as a personal challenge, a gauge if you will, to judge whether she was hitting her mark. I would get the math update as she helped him with this subject he struggled with. I would always get the "hug" update as well.

Looking back I think she really got it right. With his great brain, and years of school to come, he would eventually get the math. If we didn't teach the warmth of a hug, his life most certainly would have been quite different.

She, like me, understood the soft and subtle touch it took, to bring his chin to a neutral position, to help him look at you, as you spoke.

No guide, no advice, very little information, and with a whole lot of love and caring, we forged ahead with a depth of spirit unmatched. We had a sense of mutual purpose that would get us through. For Lisa it was a first, and would set the tone for helping future children. For me, it was the only chance I would ever have.

The first order of business was engaging his main stream teachers. Thankfully this small school in rural California was not only somewhat 'old school' in terms of ethics, it attracted many talented individuals who were looking for a highly rated school district that was progressive, paid well, and had a history of success over time.

As Lisa worked with my son, she consistently communicated with his day to day class teachers, as did I. When teachers understand parents and support staff respect their day to day engagement with a student, it becomes much easier to get that child moving forward.

As my son would attend class, always on time, always well kempt, always seemingly interested, he would occasionally "zone out". His teachers would interpret this in many different ways. Maybe too much medication? But he didn't take med's. Not enough sleep? Not a chance, as he was always in bed on time. Possibly defiance or disrespect? Not in his nature, nor tolerated by his parents.

What Lisa would pass along was, at that very moment, if they really paid attention, a train was likely going by not less than 110 yards away. A train most could hear if they paid attention, but my son heard minutes and minutes earlier as it approached.

His passion for trains was hard to "turn off" just because he was in school. I consistently and 'softly' reminded him that school was not train time. I heard from many a teacher that he very rarely brought up the subject and I was happy that this simple rule, with no explanation, was adhered to. In kind, they could certainly respect the occasional diversion as he heard the train going by.

That small close community at his elementary school was the basis for his success. My ability to engage on a regular basis and support all his teachers was not without notice, and paid off for my son.

My son did not always, if ever, communicate upcoming events and share information as some children might do. The potlucks, the field trips, the award ceremonies, all seemed to be something he didn't feel was important to bring up. I would have to rely on my 'compadres', his teachers, to understand this and make a special effort, as they did, to keep me informed. This was before e-mail, so they had my phone number and I made sure they felt comfortable using it.

The point is, as a parent of an Asperger's child it becomes your responsibility to reach out and forge relationships with the educators that could ultimately help your child down the right path to success.

Your child spends half their waking hours at school and half their waking hours at home. The more the teachers know about what is happening at home, and the more you know about what is happening at school, the better the outcome for your child.

Not only is it important for you to know what is going on at school, it is even more important that you 'support' the efforts being made to help your child be successful at school.

Don't forget, even though you have this "special little someone", namely your child, the teachers have seen hundreds of these "special little someones". They have a perspective that is invaluable, so listen.

Recently Lisa and I met to 'catch up'. My son was there too, and when she arrived the three of us engaged in the biggest, longest, "group hug" you can imagine. On a scale of one to ten on a 'hug' meter, ten being the highest, I would say we hit a twelve.

During our talk that day the subject of the train clock came up. Of course my son remembered it. I made the mistake of asking her if she still had the little train. Her eyes widened, and she leaned back slightly, as if I had just asked the stupidest question she had ever heard (yes, there are dumb questions).

I realized my error immediately. Although it had now been nearly fifteen years, and she had since transferred to another school, why would I ever, "in my wildest imagination", think she would NOT have taken along that little train.

Of course she still had that little train. I felt bad immediately and should have never begged the question. Luckily, among other things, Lisa is a very forgiving soul.

Suggestion:

Try to find that 'special' someone, whether it is special education, or mainstream staff, and partner with them. Share information about home and school, so you can support each other's efforts to help your child be comfortable in both worlds.

Chapter 4

Self 'E-Steam'

When it came to our weekends, our days off, you already know where we were likely headed. It was to the local excursion train or museum, maybe a trip to the video store. Often we would head down to Bruce's Train Store to find new and exciting things for his layout. These were always great days as we always "chatted" and had a lot of fun.

In particular there were a couple of events that I believe had a significant effect on his mind set and self-esteem. This may have been what left potential "bullies" at an impasse. Events that left him so self-assured and confident that little irritants in the school yard were so insignificant in his life I can't imagine he remembers many of them.

He excelled to such an extent in his train knowledge and expertise that, at the ripe old age of nine, he actually drove a real live locomotive. This was years ago, in a much less litigious world.

One Saturday we headed out to a local excursion train to take a ride. He of course couldn't wait to get there. All along the drive he shared his knowledge on the history of each locomotive and car, not to mention the route and details of the train schedule.

When we arrived, I discovered that for a nominal up-charge one could enjoy a ride in the engineer's cab. No-brainer there.

As we rode along in the cab, of what I was recently reminded was a GP-9 diesel number 132, the engineer began to take notice of my son's extensive knowledge of real live trains.

The engineer quizzed him with regard to every button, every control, every device, every gauge, not to mention the appropriate speed and horn signals for every crossing.

Quite satisfied this little guy was not your average train enthusiast, the engineer stood to one side of the cab chair, still running the train, and asked my son if he would like to sit in the engineer's chair.

Another "no-brainer" as my son jumped up into the chair and reveled in his new position.

He was allowed to pull the rope that controlled the horn. As we approached each crossing he confidently pulled two long's, one short, and one long which is the horn signal when approaching and moving through a crossing. My son did not disappoint, and was spot-on at every crossing.

Every engineer uses this signal but each has their own special 'style' which sets them apart. With each opportunity to pull the cord he seemed to already be forming his own special 'style'. This was extraordinary to witness and the pride I had in him, was second only to, the pride he felt himself.

Now that you know this, you will likely notice the crossing pattern if you happen to be in close proximity to a train route, and hear the horn blow.

Fast forward…A year later. I learned about what is known as "engineer-for-a-day" programs at many train related destinations. One of these programs was at a museum in fairly close proximity to our home, so I signed him up.

This museum had a track on the property large enough to allow for the running of a large diesel locomotive. A locomotive which, I have also been recently reminded, was an H-12-44 number 1487.

We arrived that day to discover a colossal warehouse. It housed multiple locomotives in various stages of reconstruction as well as disrepair. There were several massive steam trains, most of which were apparently quite famous in railroad history circles. These unbelievable steam engines are a sight to behold. The sheer size of a wheel, and the rods that rotate those wheels, makes you wonder how they ever could have built them so long ago.

As two of the Docents approached, and likely profiled us as a nice little family with a "Thomas the Train" enthusiast along…. They soon discovered, and were delightfully surprised, that our group was in fact very interested in what they had to share about "real" locomotives.

We began an ad-hoc tour, meandering around this enormous space filled with locomotives and train paraphernalia. We were constantly warned about the dangers of our surroundings, and reminded that most of the equipment could not be accessed due to treacherous conditions.

I was disappointed that we couldn't get a bit closer to some of this equipment but I understood that these Docents had their marching orders. Having driven all this way, trying to give my son the opportunity to be up close and personal with some of the very equipment he reads about, and knows every detail about, I was let down.

Then entered what I considered to be the original 'Rosie the Riveter". This gal had to be a hundred years old, if she was a day. She was clearly the "person in charge" more by default, than actual title.

She approached my son and asked him about the train he happened to be standing in front of at the time. She didn't seem a bit surprised when he began spewing out all the pertinent details. He proceeded to describe the wheel set, the traction power, the year it was built, who built it, and where it was built.

He added the years of service, and on what railroads it worked, not to mention when it was eventually taken out of service and how it landed here.

With a quick swipe of her hand, in the direction of the Docents escorting us, she led us away to a much more interesting space. As she removed the security chains and led us up into the cabs of several old steam engines, my son was in his glory. She was obviously enthralled with his knowledge. She gently questioned him on each engine and then let him speak, never forgetting to share a tidbit of information he could add to his repertoire.

I suspect she had a sense that if we didn't encourage the young ones, like my son, to stay interested in these steam engines and revere them as gems, the rich railroad past might be lost to the history books. It might be lost to the high-tech world of short term and disposable inventions.

    After all, though it's been more than a hundred years since many of these steam engines were built, many are alive and well and still operational. I definitely can't say that about the car I was driving in high school.

    Although his expertise and interest had him thoroughly enjoying the steam engines on display, he was here to drive a train. The train would be a diesel, as that was what this program offered.

    After the tour the big event of the day was imminent. He was escorted to a large diesel train and was put in the engineer's chair. The guy was quite impressed with this ten-year old, and quickly deduced the kid knew what he was doing.

    After a few instructions and a review of the safety rules, off we went. My son with a hand on the throttle and pulling the cord to sound the horn, two short toots for getting rolling.

    Sitting high on the engineer's chair, legs too short to reach the floor, he was moving the controls about as if he had been doing it for years.   He got us going along the track, slowly getting us up to speed, most assuredly a safe speed for the track that lay ahead.

His dad had traveled to meet us that day. Our little group in the cab, which included his grandma, his dad's wife and me, were most likely invisible participants to him. My son's intense joy in this activity, and his soon to be undeniable pride in the achievement, would not outweigh how impressed his little 'entourage' was that day.

I believe that building his confidence, giving him experiences that would help define him and promote self-esteem spilled over into many other aspects of his life. At that time the most significant being his school day.

Suggestion

Building self-esteem through their passion and expertise can pay off in having confidence in the other aspects of their life.

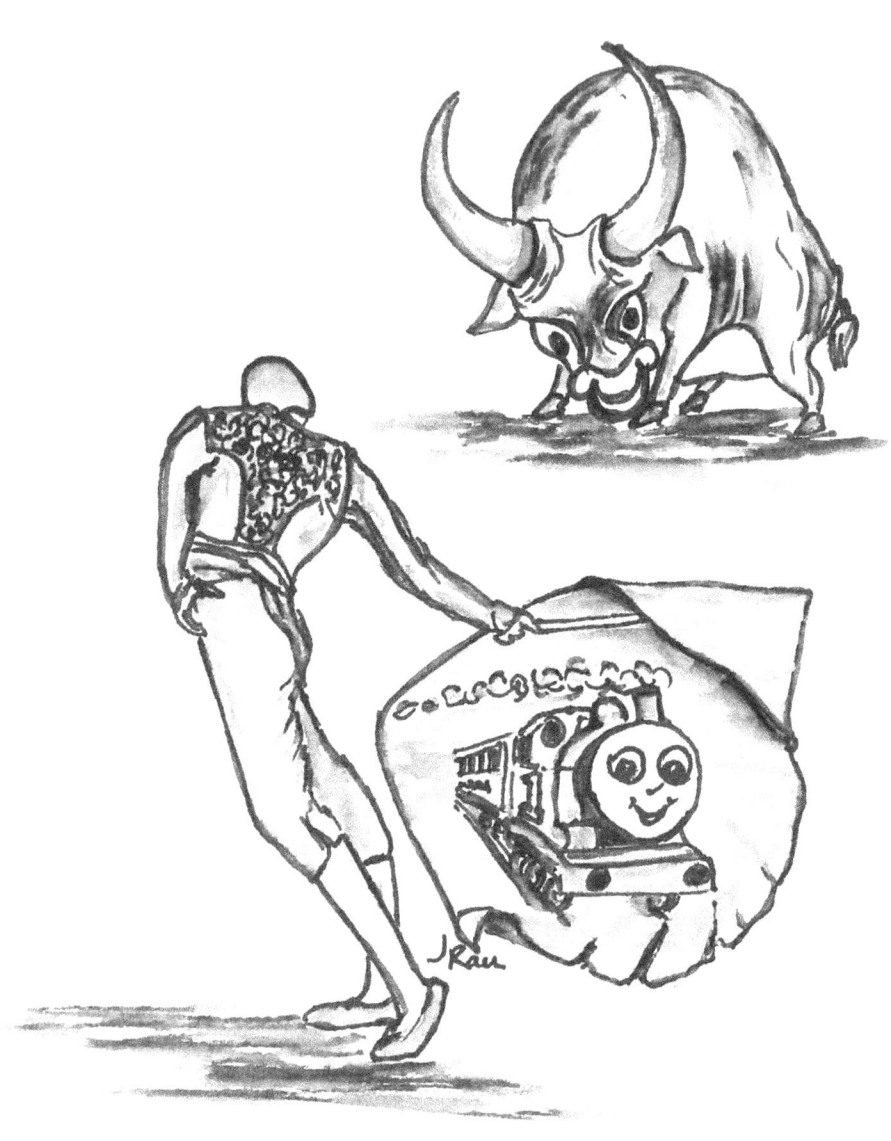

Chapter 5

"Bully for You"

Having the luxury of a small country school is like living in a small town, where everyone watches out for each other. Everyone seems to know everyone else's business, the operative phrase being 'seems' to know.

In the case of my son's elementary school, under the watchful eye of the teachers and staff, not much of what was going on in class, and on the playground, went unnoticed.

This was a school where "anti-bullying" wasn't a special program, it was just the way they 'rolled'.

Whether you have the luxury of a small school environment, or face the challenges of the organized 'chaos' the larger schools have to manage, it is wise to make your presence known as an interested and supportive parent.

Being a "kick it to the curb" and "let the school system deal with it" sort of parent, will not serve your child well. If things don't go well it becomes easy to blame everyone else, except yourself.

I know many of you might be thinking, "How the hell do I manage a full time job, a household and get active in school?" Well, as a single parent, that has a full-time job, and an entire household to manage… I'll tell you…..go to the source. Allow the teachers and the staff to know your situation.

I couldn't do the bake sales or always do the field trips…I couldn't volunteer to support the school play by sewing costumes…. But by God, I could stay active in what was going on if I allowed them to contact me at any time. I made it a point to make sure they were comfortable with getting a hold of me if there was something I needed to know or something I could reinforce to help my son in the classroom. Meeting with them for a brief chat at the end of the school day was something I did often.

Give them a phone number…an e-mail address…let them know they can contact you to discuss things. If teachers don't know who you are, can't put a face with a name, and aren't aware that you are interested in the eight hours a day your child spends with them, it is difficult at best.

When they know your situation, and your concerns, trust me, you'll have advocates all day long watching out for your child. If you take the road it is a teachers "job"...."it's what they get paid to do"...you are sadly mistaken. They are paid to 'teach'...not paid to solve underlying parenting issues that they have no control over. Although, I will say, it's amazing how many teachers are able to contribute to solving problems far beyond the reach of the classroom.

In particular, with so many parents concerned with "bullying" in our schools, my concern, having an Asperger's kid, was heightened. With my son's somewhat 'eccentric nature' I was concerned he would be an easy target for the resident bully.

Why would you send your child into an environment, give no details, and ask that a person (a teacher) discern your child's situation on their own. Wouldn't it be better to give them a 'heads up'...things to watch for, out the gate? They may come to the same conclusions, but why put them through weeks or months of discovery when you can just point things out up front.

The first important thing I did in terms of reducing the chances that my son would be bullied was to connect and have open communication with my son's teachers. This led to a security that, when I dropped him off at school, there was a host of people who I knew would watch out for him, on the playground and in the classroom. I in turn would reinforce and support their efforts on the home front.

As I continued to connect with my son's teachers, and stay engaged in his progress and activities, I became aware of an issue with another student who was apparently harassing my son. Mind you, it wasn't that he came home and complained about this student. It was more that the teachers were noticing some activity on the playground that wasn't exactly in my son's best interest.

I questioned him in a sort of 'nonchalant' manner, asking if he was having any trouble on the playground. He, of course, had nothing important to report and continued to enjoy his days at school.

At one point I was told that my son was definitely taking a beating from this little "thug in the making". It was not in the nature of the teachers, or yard duty staff, to promote retaliation, but "boy oh boy" did they obviously want to make an exception. This was for the most part verbal abuse, so lacking any physical harm, it was a difficult situation for them to address.

I became much more concerned and began to wonder what sort of effect this would have on my son emotionally. At such a young age to be picked on and made fun of could have lasting effects that would be counter- productive to the self-esteem building I promoted at home.

Enter the Asperger's mind, and sometimes lack of social graces. This was akin to a secret weapon, a secret shield, against bullies. Although this little louse was an irritant, an unwelcomed distraction to the activities on the playground, my son didn't seem to give a "rat's ass" about anything he had to say. He didn't connect any of these words as even remotely associated with reality.

Bullies thrive on getting a reaction from their intended targets. They thrive on the feeling they are getting under someone's skin. Being of "literally" sound mind and body, my son took no account of any of the nasty little instigations meant to get him to react.

This poor little bully was getting no results. My son's inaction and lack of understanding that this kid's words were intended as a social put down, was shutting this 'little shit' down.

I knew the teachers and staff watched for any 'physical' abuse, but other than that…there probably wasn't a whole lot to worry about.

Lack of social graces can sometimes save someone from feeling bullied as it doesn't necessarily occur to them that what another person is 'saying' is really important. Especially if the words make no sense or aren't true.

The second most important aspect of my son's shield to potential bullies was my promoting his interest in other things not related to school. His activities outside of school, especially in relation to train matters, helped him to form an appropriate and balanced view of himself.

Even though school was the top-priority in our household, it was by no means the only priority. Family, household chores, outside activities and trips were also a priority in living a "well rounded" life.

Celebrating and admiring his knowledge and expertise on all things trains must have given him a good 'sense' about himself. I can't imagine it's any different than a soccer player or little 'leaguer' getting accolades from parents and family for a great play, or an extra effort that helped win the game.

Bottom line, keeping an active life, inclusive of his passion, built his confidence. This confidence spilled over into his school life. It would help him be successful at school and help him to avoid the pit falls of falling prey to a bully.

Suggestion

Connect with teachers and staff, let them be your "eyes and ears" and celebrate your child's expertise on the home front.

Chapter 6

"Tattling the Truth"

Being an avid reader, and a huge fan of Stephen King, I was entrenched one evening in one of his scary, surreal novels. As I was reading, I came to a description of a conversation his protagonist was having with his friend and travel mate. In signature Stephen King style, he captures this conversation in such vivid detail, you feel as if you could actually be there as a silent witness.

During this conversation the main character is put in a rather uncomfortable position and feels compelled to, what the author describes as, "tattling the truth".

I was taken aback. That term jumped right out of the pages and hit me like "a ton of bricks". Tattling the truth was a perfect way to describe what my son did on occasion.

Out of nowhere, he would announce exactly what he was thinking, whether or not it was the right time or place for his comments. In private, I could take it in stride. In public, it could sometimes result in awkward situations.

Not unlike their eye contact, our Asperger's literal thinkers are fairly easy to detect. They have a natural talent for telling the truth at all times, even if it's not quite the right time or place.

Sometimes his comments were so painfully and obviously correct, that I welcomed it as "comic relief" and put it to the back of my mind. I felt that stressing over every little comment he made wasn't going to amount to anything.

There were times I would secretly want to give him a "high-five" because what he said would be exactly what I was thinking. He was saying what I didn't have the courage to say. So caught up in the social nuances, I sometimes missed opportunities to speak my mind. Although, most people who know me, will find that extremely hard to believe.

The best example was his unwavering belief that all small children should get whatever they ask for, whatever they want. When he was faced with children at the market in the checkout counter, begging their mom for a candy bar, if she said 'no', he had absolutely no problem directly addressing this mom, and quite boldly asking her, "why can't they have candy"?

    The kids would react by looking at their mom and waiting for her answer.   The mom would usually react with a stern look in my direction, identifying me as the mother of this ill-mannered child. I would react by maneuvering my son to a more distant position from the situation, but secretly be wondering the same thing.

    Based on her grocery basket of goodies, I would assess the situation and profile accordingly. If there was an ample supply of cookies and ice cream along with the ingredients for meals and household needs I might apologize. Clearly she had already supplied her little brood with treats. I suspected that with each new aisle traveled, there was, yet again, something they just "had to have". Now that she was at the checkout counter she was likely thinking "enough is enough."

    If she had a grocery cart full of clearly thought out, cost conscience dinner ingredients, when her child had asked for just one thing I would wonder why she couldn't simply carve out just one quarter for this one small item, as my son had suggested. Then behind her, as her older set of twins arrived, with another little brother and sister in tow, I realized that if everyone was allowed even one small thing, the total price could exceed what she might pay for an entire meal.

If she was what I call a "fly-by" mom she had a cart that included a 12-pack of beer, a bucket of chicken from the deli, a container of potato salad, and some lunchables. At first glance one might wonder why she couldn't trade the 12-pack for a 6-pack and succumb to her children's wishes. But, it was just as likely that she had a house full of painters, her kitchen was torn apart and not in any condition that could accommodate cooking, and the 12-pack was an offering to hopefully get these guys out of the house a.s.a.p.

I wouldn't have to worry about an apology from any 'fly-by' mom. She was usually so hell bent on getting through the check- out line and out the door I doubted she had even heard her children's request for the candy bar. Even less likely that she had heard my son's comment that their wish should be granted.

Either way, judgments aside, it is important that we slowly and patiently teach that even honesty comes at a price. What appears to be one-way, could certainly be quite the opposite.

The price we pay at the expense of others, as we grow and learn, is that things may not always be what they appear. We have to try to keep an open mind, and not judge too harshly. This is a tough concept to teach a literal thinker like my son, especially one so young. This is also a tough concept to teach to others, when they encounter my son.

These are instances where it's important that we follow through with social graces, as people's feelings might get hurt. Although telling the truth is an indicator of stellar moral character, there are times when for social reasons we have to teach our child to hold back. Not to lie !....just to hold back.

When we have spent so much time and energy just getting these kids to communicate and then have to strategize on how we teach them when and how to communicate, it can be a very slippery slope.

When an awkward situation did occur, I would run myself through a short series of questions.
Will I ever see these people again? If no...'screw it', just move on.
Was anyone physically or emotionally hurt? If no.....just move on.
If it was a family member or neighbor, I told them I was "working on it".

More importantly, this would never fall under the category of punishment. I had spent too much time and effort to make sure my son was not silent. Admonishing him now for speaking carried a risk that he might fall silent once again.

Fortunately or unfortunately, depending on your view, my son would eventually mature and better understand the social nuances, namely, when tattling the truth isn't always the best course of action. Never lie, but sometimes just choose to have no comment.

I have faith that someday, at some point, he like other men will be faced with the most dreaded question of all, from the woman he loves…and that is "Does my ass look fat in these jeans?"

If I raised him properly, he will have the right answer, regardless.

Suggestion

Deal with each situation diplomatically. Rather than punishment, use it as a 'teachable moment'.

Chapter 7

R-E-S-P-E-C-T

Although some of you may not be familiar with, or remember this...
There's a great song from the past by Aretha Franklin titled "Respect". If you're not familiar with this rendition please go to 'You Tube' and check it out.

The artist belts out a song using seven letters to describe a concept that we seem sometimes to have forgotten about. That concept is a simple one, one we need to apply to other...and that is R-E-S-P-E-C-T.

We all loved the song for her resounding voice, the beat and melody, and most important, the message of respect. (Although, I never really did get the "sock it to me" part?)

My son attended a local elementary school, and like Aretha, they clearly promoted respect as an underlying value. The design of the school curriculum fostered a culture of inclusion.

This culture of inclusion reached out to the diverse population they dealt with on a daily basis, well before there was legislation that instructed them to do so. They had very large classes, mainstreamed special education students, and dealt with the challenges of students who were only accustomed to speaking English at school.

This little elementary school dealt with a diverse middle class, as well as kids from a labor force that tended to the fields in the vicinity. From kids who barely had breakfast and made it to school on time, to kids who had been up for hours helping with the cows or horses, or both.

There were teachers who provided morning snacks, as there were no programs at the time for kids that clearly needed a jump start to their day. A cafeteria staff that had no problem making a plate for a child that seemed to have 'forgotten' their lunch.

If a child showed up at the cash register, pulling out a handful of nickels and dimes, it was amazing how it was always "just enough" to pay for the meal they had ordered.

These were teachers and staff that clearly communicated regarding the little individuals they had in their charge for eight hours a day.

You may think you don't enjoy the same trappings as I did, but you might be surprised. All these sorts of things could be going on "right under your nose". Unless you are open to it…you may never see it.

All during my son's school years I promoted first and foremost respect for the teachers and staff at school. I wanted to make certain he understood he was "the kid"…he was "the student"…and the teachers were there to support him and help him along…they were "in charge". He was there, in turn, to respect his teachers by listening, doing what he was asked to do, and learning as much as he possibly could from them.

I started from one basic premise, one underlying value, which is 'most' people are good. Therefore, since teachers are people, most teachers must be good. Likewise, 'some' people are bad, teachers are people, and therefore 'some' teachers are bad. It's basically the old "80/20" rule.

I can't help but think that our educators, based on their experiences, apply this same sort of logic to the student and parent population they serve.

Since young children for the most part follow their parents lead, I did my best to support and collaborate with his teachers regarding classroom activities, homework and projects. My son being aware, that "I" was aware, encouraged him to participate and follow through with assignments both in class and outside of class. If something did come up that I questioned, believe me, those same teachers were open to a discussion as I wasn't the proverbial parent who only showed up to complain.

If you participate when things are going well, try to be involved and support a teachers efforts as much as possible, when something does come up that you question, you are more likely to be heard because you have been, historically, a positive support system for a teacher. Ergo…teachers are people too.

With an Asperger's child in particular, it is likely that you are only getting a "tiny piece of the pie" with regard to what went on during the school day. In order to glean more accurate information about what occurs at school, you have to stay connected with the teachers as much as possible.

During the formative elementary school years, children don't need to be exposed to every aspect of their parent's 'adult views'. When something does come up at school that you want to address, it isn't necessary that you directly communicate or share that concern with your child, who may not fully understand the issue.

If you come across information that doesn't sit quite right with you, you need to first investigate. This is not the time to throw a hissy fit about what you "think" might be going on. Take a deep breath, and short of bruises, get the facts before you react.

If you do have to approach a teacher or principal regarding an issue, try to do so with a question rather than an accusation. What you may find is the teacher or the principal is already aware of the issue and dealing with it. Then it becomes an opportunity, once again, to respect and support each other for the benefit of your child.

When my son reached 5th grade I already suspected a potential for problems. His class was being "team taught" by two teachers, each of whom only wanted to work part time. The school district calls this arrangement a 'shared contract' and each teacher alternates based on a prearranged schedule.

As he thrived in a more predictable environment, one with continuity on a day to day basis, I anticipated problems for him, but respected that other students might not be adversely affected.

These two teachers came up with what I consider to be a "hare-brained" idea. By trading off days, and carefully coordinating the curriculum, it was possible for the students to get all they needed during that year. Further, the fact that a principal would approve this arrangement, which seemed obviously flawed, surprised me at the time. I kept an open mind, didn't complain out the gate, but I did have concerns.

Unlike when my sister and I attended elementary school years and years before, with one teacher and one classroom a constant all year long, these kids were already being shuffled from class to class on different days and at different times. I hoped for the best for my son that year, as there was no choice.

I didn't really understand how a teacher, educated at the college level, wouldn't have the ability to teach grade level reading, writing, math, science and history, but that was just how it was now. With specialty subjects like Computers, it was probably best to have a focused teacher, and my son most likely benefited from having an expert in each area.

He was also, most likely, better prepared for the transition to middle school, where he would be expected to change classrooms every hour, all day long.

Each morning the students would report to their primary teacher, in a designated classroom. These homeroom teachers would have to be well versed on which students were to be sent off to what classroom, on what days, and at what times, to enjoy the full benefit of a focused teacher on a particular subject.

In the course of this 5th grade "team taught" year, one day I received a somewhat unnerving report. On this particular day my son had been found alone, in the back of his classroom, under a desk.

He was discovered by a teacher who noticed he was missing from class. A class that was part of my son's regularly scheduled routine. This was a student who never missed school, and seemed to always be where he ought to be, so this teacher went to find him....and of course, did.

Let's recap the day this incident occurred. There are more than twenty students, dealing with one of 'two' possible teachers. In addition, based on what day of the week it was and what time it was, each student needed to be sent to the right classroom for their respective 'focused' subject.

Add, as in my son's case, the possibility of a scheduled session with a speech therapist or specialist, a session that had hopefully been communicated in advance to the teacher 'du jour'.

Given that scenario, I'm actually surprised he wasn't abandoned in the back of the class under a desk more often.

That particular day was cloudy, dark, and gloomy. Once told about the incident, I pictured my son in an unlit classroom, alone and probably wondering what was going on. Before coming 'un-glued' I gathered the facts.

My son appeared to be in good order, and ready to jump in the car and go home. It was his teacher who reported the incident to me, so there was no 'hiding' the fact, even in the unlikely event my son might actually share it with me. Most important, the error was caught fairly quickly by an astute teacher, which confirmed that they were watching over my son.

Now that other teachers, and I'm sure the principal, were aware of the issue and probably had the same concerns about this "team teaching" experiment, was there really a need to march into the principal's office to add my 'two cents'? Probably not.

More importantly, was it necessary for me to share with my son the fact that his teachers had dropped the ball? Did I need to rip them apart, or share the information with someone else within his earshot? Absolutely not.

This was the 20% of the 80/20 rule. Not everything that happens will turn out well, but the minute you start sharing your concerns directly with your child, or with someone else in your child's presence, you run the risk of undermining the authority of the folks who are in charge of them half of their waking hours.

The wisdom of promoting respect for teachers, and their authority, isn't only valuable from an educational perspective. What about your child's safety?

In the unlikely event there is a crisis, don't you want to make sure your kids have been taught to listen and 'mind' the teacher? Taught to do what the teacher says and go where the teacher tells them to go?

You have every right to voice your concerns when issues arise. You have every right to discuss these concerns with the school or with others. However, the minute you include your child in the mix, you may be undermining your child's ability to respect teachers and the authority they represent. This could strip your child of the opportunity to get the most out all of the many talented educators they will encounter in the future.

That day as we drove home I kindly and gently asked my son about his day. I asked him about being alone in the classroom. He didn't appear traumatized and didn't seem upset about the day. I asked him why he ended up in his classroom alone, under a desk. His response was that his teacher had told him, if there was ever a disaster, he should crawl under a desk and wait.

Working hard to keep my chuckle to a mere smirk, remembering my own earthquake safety training so many years ago, I thought to myself, "only in California."

Suggestion

Staying connected to the teachers and staff in the good times…. will help in the "not so good' times.

Chapter 8

Rubik's Cube Parenting

"If you are curious, you'll find the puzzles around you. If you are determined, you will solve them".

Erno Rubik
Inventor of the Rubik's Cube

I once read that, without instruction, it is almost impossible to solve the Rubik's Cube puzzle. It can be an infuriating, yet engaging, task. It requires a high level of intelligence, yet the confusion experienced along the way can make someone feel like a real dummy.

This is how I often felt as I raised my son. There were times when what I was doing seemed to make sense, yet the outcome wasn't quite what I expected. I would have to go back and re-visit things trying things at random that ended up working, for some unknown reason.

My son had mastered 5th grade disaster preparedness, now it was off to 6th grade. I continued to lack any sort of concrete instructions on how best to face each challenge. Just like with any other kid, as my son matured, adjustments would need to be made as life expanded on many fronts.

I was facing new situations and new challenges but persisted with the same overall strategy which I now dub the Rubik's Cube style of parenting. If something wasn't working, I would step back, re-think things, view things from a new vantage point and try a different approach.

My need to continue to control the environment around him, not believing he was ready to fend for himself, may have seemed a problem for some. For us, day to day life was less complex that way. Setting him up for success was, in my opinion, the most important function I served at the time.

In 6th grade I continued most of the routines from previous years, not concerned yet with what would need adjusting after he moved on from elementary school. After all, he WAS still in elementary school.

Clothes were laid out the night before, making sure pants and shirts matched. Depending on whether it was fall or spring, the appropriate jacket or sweatshirt put by the front door. Lunch was packed and in the refrigerator, ready to be squeezed into the 40-pound backpack he hauled to school.

Proceeding down a bit of a "rabbit hole"…I have to say that damn back- pack irritated the hell out of me. In my day the only people who carried back packs were seasoned hikers, sportsman, and the occasional free-spirited hippie.

My generation didn't get the pleasure of wearing this 40 lb. tool until we attended college. Up until then, we carried our books or used lockers. I'll have to ask my folks how they possibly survived and emerged as thinking, educated people without a back pack in tow.

At the end of his 6th grade year all the parents and extended family were invited to the promotion ceremony. Thankfully, this was a time when we didn't have to worry about finding caps and gowns 'prematurely'. This was an appropriate ceremony with everyone dressed as they would any other school day. The only difference being, instead of attending class that day, the students were asked to help set up all the chairs and decorations for their families.

I'm hearing that kindergartners now have a ceremony with caps and gowns.
You absolutely do NOT want to hear my opinion on that...it might turn into another entire book.

Heading back to the subject at hand......I left work early that day and arrived at the 6th grade promotion in the late morning. It was a beautiful sunny day, not too hot, and no wind. I personally am not a fan of wind.

I met up with my mom and dad and we maneuvered through the folding chairs. All of the chairs had been set up in a grassy area that was fairly unstable due to heavy watering. We were trying to find chairs that were firmly grounded.

I'm sure there were instructions in advance not to water, but what is more likely is the event had been moved at the last minute from the multi-purpose room to this outside area. After all, where were the 1st through 5th graders going to have lunch?

My mom and I smiling, my dad seemingly uninterested but too nosey not to attend, we found our seats. The ceremonies soon commenced.

To kick off the ceremony was our principal. That lady was a real piece of work, in more ways than one. The cost of an outfit she might wear on a

Monday would easily have paid for my wardrobe the entire week. She didn't walk, she 'strutted'.

When you heard the 'click, click, click' of her heels coming up the hallway behind you, you did a silent little prayer as she passed. That little prayer was giving thanks to the powers that be, that you were not her intended target. You were not going to be at the receiving end of whatever mission she was on that day.

That being said, she was also 'one hell of a principal'! She ran a tight ship. Many of the things I loved most about that school were surely the result of a leadership style that trickled down.

She seemed to have eyes in the back of her head, and if I didn't know better, given the technology at the time, I would swear she had a hidden camcorder in every classroom.

It was clear on that day she didn't need a roster to introduce each and every student.

We heard from teachers, students, and a district 'big wig'. Late morning turned into early afternoon and as the temperature rose I began wondering why I wasn't a fan of, maybe not wind, but at least a small breeze.

We appreciated when the principal announced what would now be the culmination of the ceremony, namely, the Presidential Awards. I knew that shortly it would be time to meet up with my son, and pack it in.

As we listened to descriptions of students whose names I was so familiar with, clapping as they received their awards, I also searched among the crowd to get a glimpse of their parents and their pride.

From academic achievement, to science and technology, to personal success, each student was recognized for their outstanding achievement.

My son's 6th grade teacher was introduced and walked to the podium. She proceeded to describe a student who seemed to have an unmatched desire to succeed, even when it meant having to try and try again.

As some kids get things right out the gate, and others give up if they don't succeed the first time, the student she described always kept trying until they got it "right". My dad, mom, and I glanced at each other, with mutual understanding of the value of this particular child's achievement. This was not merely a 6th grade achievement, but recognition of child's intrinsic nature, and how that would help carry them through life.

Now imagine that same glance when his 6th grade teacher called out my son's name. It was not only surprise, it was elation! It was an emotional moment that brought tears to my eyes.

It was also a moment when I had just learned something about my own son, that I had never known before.

With all the day to day taking care of business, my son never really had to fall short at anything on the home front. He never really had to try and try again, because I would support any cause for him to get it right, without the feeling of failure.

Out here in the world, it would sometimes be others who recognized something in him that I didn't see myself. That day a teacher was recognizing a personality trait that didn't come up at home, because I didn't allow it to.

Although I continued to take care of most things, I now looked at him from a different perspective. I was able to let go of some things and have him try to handle more things on his own. I knew it was 'o.k.' if he failed at something the first time out, realizing now he wouldn't need much encouragement to try again, as that was his nature.

Some people seem to just sail through to success. For most of us, success is often preceded by an ample supply of perseverance.

Stepping back, and looking at my little Rubik's Cube from a new angle, helped me support him on a whole new level. It would ultimately help lead to many of the successes coming in the future.

Suggestion

Be open to what others see in your child. Add that knowledge to help solve the puzzles you encounter.

Chapter 9

The Safety Net

As my son had now made his way through elementary school, it was time to venture closer to the "big leagues" of high school. On the way he would have to endure a short stint in the triple AAA's, better known as middle school. I was not looking forward to it.

He would have additional chores at home, and after a short period of confusion, in conjunction with some training, he would learn new tasks, and gain a new pride in all the things he could do himself. I would have to work on "allowing" him to have the responsibilities. I would set the days, times and expectations, but I had to learn to step back and not go behind him to fix anything.

Being a person, like myself, who was comfortable with predictable and rote routines, he seemed to find it fairly easy to take care of the duties I had outlined. I don't recall that I had to remind him much. Among other things he always remembered to make his bed every morning, feed the cat at 6PM, and take out the trash before it overflowed.

Being well aware there would no longer be bake sales, Christmas productions, or field trips where I could tag along, I would have to create a new plan on how to stay in touch with what went on at school. No longer would I be able to saunter onto the school grounds after school and be free to seek out a teacher to touch base with.

Although my son and I communicated a bit more, I was aware that 'pertinent' information would likely continue to be left out. I was also painfully aware there wouldn't be the close attention paid during recess, as there was no recess now. The teachers wouldn't necessarily question if he wasn't in class that day.

Given there were more than five feeder schools, and this was a very large middle school campus, a lot would go on that wasn't under the direct supervision of the teachers and staff. What went on in the hallways, and restrooms, during the 12 minutes between classes would be largely unattended, as the teachers and staff were in their classrooms preparing for the next group.

Luckily there had been some coordination between the elementary school and the middle school regarding the students involved in what our school district called the 'Strategies Program'. This was a group of students of vastly different needs, lumped into one category. These were students who needed some form of additional support during their school day.

We are talking about a "soup to nuts" group. From students who might need one-on-one physical support, to students who needed to remain in a single classroom the entire day. Some who needed oversight, getting them to the right place at the right time, to those who merely needed someone to check in with each day.

During the first week of school, parents were invited to meet with the coordinator of the strategies program. This meeting was set up at the coordinators discretion. If you couldn't come in on the designated day and time you were S.O.L.

I found a way to adjust my schedule and get to that meeting. I was wrong to assume that the time I allowed to drive there, and park in the schools adjacent-lot, was more than enough time to get to the scheduled meeting.

I ended up having to park blocks away in a residential area as the school parking lot was full of cars, all lined up with no room to spare between them. I made my way to the office to check in and receive what I assumed would be the required visitor's badge. I was wrong again.

The office was ten times the size of the elementary school office, I now so sorely missed. No one seemed to care who I was, or what I needed.

I was finally able to flag someone down to ask directions to the particular room number I had been told to report to, nearly 10 minutes ago.

I was sent packing with a vague idea of where I was going. I was told to exit the back door, turn left, head down the hallway to the end, make a right, and by continuing on, I would find that room.

As I exited the back door the spike in the decibel level was immediate. It reminded me of being at Qualcomm Stadium years before when the San Diego Chargers had just scored the final goal that would take us to the playoffs.

As excited as I was about those playoff games, I had mixed emotions. I calculated that according to the schedule, I would be dragging my 'lard- ass' up the stairs, to our season ticket seats, at right about 8 months pregnant.

I did in fact make it to that playoff game, and did get up the stairs to my seat. Unfortunately the Chargers fell to the Colts that day. Although my son was not classified as premature, he did come a few weeks early. Do the math.

Any way, I finally found my way to the right room. As I entered I was immediately intimidated when this gentleman took a long, intentionally delayed, glance at the clock. He made his point. I, being always on time or early, was already put in a defensive position, but I let it go with no comment.

As I walked forward to shake hands and introduce myself, he stood up from his chair and towered over me by more than a foot, but it seemed like two. This guy reminded me of a guy I dated in college when I was in my "biker chick" phase. Tack on several years, a red bandana, a jeans jacket, and put him on a Harley, he could surely be one and the same.

After this brief "flashback" I did introduce myself. He went on to confirm my son's name, assuring that we were the right two people in the room.

His robust name matched his robust style. He had an eastern European last name that was difficult to pronounce and even more difficult to spell. Because his name was too cumbersome for many of his students, he insisted on being called, simply, Mr. 'H'.

By sharing that he was comfortable with being called Mr. H, made me feel like I might possibly get in "the club" someday. He talked briefly about my son, and had already pegged me as the overprotective mom, that I of course was.

He didn't make me feel guilty, or try to change my mind, he just assured me that things would be fine and made it clear it would be more of a "Don't call me, I'll call you" arrangement.

Don't get me wrong. I don't mean to depict him as a stern individual. Mr. H is more of a 'commanding' individual. He is clear to a fault. His style instills a confidence that he knows exactly "what the doctor ordered", not only for his students but for parents as well.

We talked a bit more about his program. I briefly outlined some of my perspectives. This seemed to assure him I was obviously a fan of teachers. He let down a little, and there ended up being a bit of comic relief when he shared a story about the "parents from hell". I felt confident he had already removed me from that list.

Mr. H doesn't have a laugh that is contagious. It is more of a deep sincere laugh that you witness and absorb. You may not be laughing 'with' him but, because his laugh is so entertaining, you still find yourself laughing anyway.

As the year progressed, and meetings were few and far between, the time flew by. I picked up my son each day and grew accustomed to parking next to a young woman that also had a boy to pick up. She and I would acknowledge each other with a short wave and smile.

Our two boys would walk out together most days. These two boys were about as opposite in stature and style as you can get. My son, in addition to being a bit below average height at the time, also had the lean body we hate when we're young, but long for as we age. His buddy on the other hand, was taller than all his peers and many of his teachers. He, more likely than not, outweighed most of the junior varsity football squad at the high school they both would soon be attending.

One day I picked up my son and had the energy to engage in the Q & A style of conversation we tended to have. Since he would not typically offer any information, I would have to ask a series of short specific questions in order to discern the information I was looking for.

I asked him how is day was. He answered, "good". I asked him who the boy he walked out with was. He answered "my buddy". I asked him how he met his buddy. He answered Mr. H's class.

Soon after this chat, I arrived a bit early to pick up my son, and actually found a parking spot. I didn't have to park next to a red curb, engine running, anticipating the mass exodus.

I noted that the young woman, who typically picked up my son's new friend, had just pulled up. With several minutes to spare, and no need to idle near the curb, I decided to take our relationship beyond a smile and a wave. I was curious to hear her story and find out what she might know about this new found friendship.

I locked my car and walked to her vehicles driver side. It was very hot that day. The first few months of our school year are also, technically, the last few months of summer. At this time of year the thermometer can easily read over 100 degrees by the time school lets out.

As I approached she was forced to roll down the window of her air conditioned vehicle to greet me, but didn't seem to mind. She left the engine running which gave her a bit of cool air. I was already feeling the tiny beads of sweat that seem to roll down the back of your neck, right behind your ears, the minute the mercury rises over 90.

We introduced ourselves and I observed she appeared too young to have a boy in middle school. We exchanged small bits of informative personal information. She was apparently not the boy's mother but was his aunt. She was the wife of this boy's older brother.

Based on her current schedule, she had become the designated driver after school. This was obviously a family that took everything into account and made decisions based on the entire family's mutual needs.

She knew my son's name and indicated his buddy would always include him in a description of his day at school. Boy, wouldn't I love to have that sort of detail!

Nonetheless, now that I knew my son had a buddy, I could incorporate that knowledge into our frequent Q & A sessions. By including his friend "in the mix" during these interrogations, I was able to glean much more information about what actually went on that day at school.

If I asked what he and his buddy did that day I would be more likely to hear about the goings on at lunch, since they ate lunch together most days. If I questioned, "What did you guys do today?", I was more likely to hear about their attendance at a rally or school event.

How these two boys got together and became pals, both his mom and I later suspected, had something to do with Mr. H. It would make perfect sense that if Mr. H had orchestrated this "buddy system" he too would be kept better informed, and be promoting a safer environment for both boys.

Strangely enough, although each of them had very distinct cultural surnames, they had the same initials. Even more quirky was that alphabetically they were always right next to each other on a roster. Sometimes I wonder if Mr. H didn't simply draw a random line for his buddy system.

Whether it was divine intervention, or Mr. H's strategy protocols, it didn't matter. Although there may have been a bit of planning and foresight in getting these guys together, the collateral benefit would be the formation of a very close friendship that stood the test of time. My son and his buddy would eventually take different paths, but to this day, they stay in touch.

In addition to this "team" approach, Mr. H made it very clear to his students that if they ever got in a bind, ever got caught in a predicament they couldn't sort out, there was a "safe zone" to go to. Whether it be the strategies classroom or his office, everyone knew the plan, knew where they would go if anything bad happened.

I would also suspect that teachers were informed that if they ran into any difficult situations with their mainstreamed strategies students, they too had a way to get their student to the right place. If they ran into a something they were not familiar with, or trained to deal with, it was "A OK" to send their student to this safe place.

All in all, we muddled through the challenges of middle school. My son continued to do well in school, but now, as I had not looked forward to middle school, I looked forward even less to high school. Yet, the thrill that he was moving on was exciting.

My mom met me at the school on the day of the 8th grade graduation. It was a zoo. I'm surprised we even found one another, and we never did find any seats. I don't believe we actually ever saw my son or heard his name called.

After the ceremony, my mom headed out, and I was left pacing the parking lot, hoping my son would find me.

At that moment Mr. H drove by, and stopped. He wasn't on the Harley I always pictured him on, but was driving an "off road" type of vehicle with the dirt and grime indicating his priorities were in the right place during the school year. I imagined that after a road trip he got home just in time to put together a lesson plan and sort out what his week might look like. The last of his worries would be making sure his vehicle was 'spic and span'.

He let me know that my son would be coming out shortly. He assured me that my son would likely go straight to the office if he was unable to locate me.

I often wondered if he hadn't been himself lurking, making sure I was there. Without a doubt he had already provided my son with a plan for getting to a "safe place".

Suggestion
Make sure your child has a plan, and is comfortable executing the plan. Find a teacher who will help your child to secure a buddy, have a place to go for lunch, and have an exit strategy when things get confusing.

Chapter 10

Staying Off the 'Pity-Pot'

Although at times it was taxing, I was pleased to be raising my son in a household that consisted of, just us. Having the ability to focus on him and provide a predictable environment helped to keep things calm.

I truly don't know how parents with multiple children manage, even when it's a two parent household. Just the logistics of packing lunches, hoping for enough clean underwear for everyone, not to mention assuring homework is done and making sure there is enough time for everyone to have breakfast, must be overwhelming.

I imagine when the kids are all young and attending the same school it is less challenging. I can't fathom how inconvenient it must be as they grow, each one needing to get to a totally different location, possibly at the same time, each day.

It's not that there wasn't a lot of activity in our small household. The neighborhood kid's visits after school were manageable and welcomed, but you could always just send them home when it was time.

Family gatherings and holidays often occurred at my house as I love to cook. The events were planned in advance, and I could prepare my son.

Most important, when things did go south, and I had to deal with a meltdown, it was much easier to deal with this crisis one-on-one, just my son and me. I didn't have the burden of someone else in the mix. A person who might try to intervene, likely, making things worse.

I didn't have to deal with the judgment from others that all parents experience when their child is behaving badly. Whether it is a person in the store, or your own damn family, people look at isolated, event-related, incidents as always being the result of bad parenting.

Staying on course with avoiding medication, using wit, logic and lots of perseverance instead, there were still times when things could get quite physical.

When he was young and small, my size and strength were enough. As he got older..... not so much.

As my son moved through pre-teen and early teen years I came to realize that his "feelings" were not that much different from his peers. What differed was, that not always being able to communicate his feelings, his frustrations and emotions might present themselves in a more physical way.

As he matured, as the communication skills improved for both of us, there might be stressful events, but the sheer magnitude was greatly reduced. Generally he was a very polite, well mannered young man who was very concerned with those around him. When he was frustrated, his emotions could spill over, but as he aged he was able to return to his typical character more quickly.

It's a bit of a mystery that along the way, as I dealt in isolation with many issues, for the most part I remained stoic. I had good days and bad, just like everyone else, yet I remained upbeat and energetic, not allowing myself to wish for anything else than what I had.

Part of my routine was to read the daily newspaper. Sometimes I had a moment in the morning but more often I would read the paper on and off while I was preparing dinner. Scanning just the front page alone, exposed me to the dismal state of affairs, and catastrophic events, going on in the world.

It was sad, sometimes depressing, to see stories about people who were really hurting out there. I couldn't directly relate to their strife but more often than not, it caused that inner voice in me to "thank my lucky stars". The things I read about in relation to other people's lives, made my life look like 'a piece of cake'.

During a tough time, it was easier to "pull up my boot straps" and move on when I reminded myself of something that another human being had faced. Reminding myself that my situation paled in comparison to what many other people had to deal with.

I also had exposure to a subset of society that I became directly involved with. For every student in my son's strategies program there was of course an associated parent or parent(s), dealing with their own set of difficulties.

Thanks to my son's buddy, I had the honor of meeting some of the most wonderful people I have ever met. The first big event was a gathering at his buddy's house to celebrate his birthday. My son received an invitation which also included me.

Not knowing what to expect, I was happy this was a mid-day event. The time on the invitation indicated food would not necessarily be a focus. It might just be a cake and B-Day presents event? Boy was I wrong.

My son and I set out that Saturday to the address on the invitation and I was surprised at how quickly we arrived. They actually lived very close to us. We were right on time, not 'fashionably' late. I feared we might be the first arrivals but as we turned onto the court in question, there was not a parking space in sight.

We parked on a side street and walked to the large two story house at the end of the court. We could hear the catchy beat of the music blasting from the back of the house. As we approached the front door, we couldn't miss the "COME IN" sign, obviously thrown together as a response to a constant barrage of doorbell rings.

Walking through the door into a living area that was empty, it was obvious the party was out in back. As I glanced to the left I saw a dining room with a table that seated at least twelve. On that table was a display of culinary delights, none of which could possibly have been purchased at the local deli.

This was home cooked food reflecting a well thought out menu which took into account any and all cultures who might venture through the front door.

There were all the fixin's for hamburgers and hot dogs which were likely grilling in the back, based on the aroma as we walked in the door. There was chicken and ribs, obviously grilled a bit earlier to be ready for consumption now. There were several types of beans and salads, to complement anyone's choice of main dish.

And there it was, at the back of the table, the most lumpia I had ever seen in one place, at one time. Also, next to this mountain of lumpia were several little 'lakes', all full of the most wonderful sauces associated with this delicacy.

We ventured through a doorway, into the kitchen. We were immediately greeted by his buddy's mom. She introduced her own mom, who was at the stove continuing to cook additional lumpia. Wow!

She introduced us to her other son's, and to their wives, various cousins, possibly aunts….maybe neighbors?.. She took me around to meet the other parents as my son escaped to the back yard.

I was urged to get some food, and a drink from one of the ice chests on the back patio. As I ventured out the screen door there was an immediate aroma of what I consider to be the best grilled meat I've ever tasted.

Next to the grill providing hot dogs and burgers to whomever showed up with the appropriate bun, was another barbecue grill filled with sticks loaded with a thin cut marinated meat, the likes of which I had never tasted. It was manned by a gentleman who was obviously the resident dad.

I am usually more of a 'talker' than an 'eater', but on that day I found the biggest plate I could find, and on it, I strategically placed pieces of each of the delights I had encountered. I pulled my son away for a moment and had him fill up a plate as well. We found a bench seat on the back patio which gave me time to eat, but also gave me time to sit back and "observe".

What I saw in "all their glory", was a large, extended family, who was quite used to putting together an event. Hell, given the size of the family, and the size of the dining room table, their regular dinner time would be considered an 'event' for most of us.

There was suddenly a commotion. The kids were up and moving, like a school of fish, towards the side-yard. As I turned to see what was going on, there he was, Mr. H. He began to laugh along with all the kids gathering around him. He was like the Pied Piper, and those kids surely would have followed him anywhere.

It was so great to see him again. My son had moved on from middle school so I just assumed I would never see Mr. H again. We spoke, and he was genuinely thrilled that my son and his buddy were friends that had obviously stood the test of time.

This day marked the beginning of a friendship and the formation of relationships that would be very influential for both my son and I, for the next several years. On that day I met some of most wonderful kids, some of the most challenged kids I would ever meet.

This, like other events that followed, would be a "soft spot" to land. I wouldn't have to worry about where my son was, or what he said, or what people would think. Likewise, the other parents could all relax knowing they were in an environment of complete acceptance, complete understanding and complete support.

Although our children's diagnosis could be polar opposites, the lifestyle we shared could be amazingly similar. When I was faced with the sheer physical challenges of some of these kids, and the cognitive challenges of others, I was humbled.

One of my favorites was a kid that, for all his physical issues, was one of the happiest most uplifting people I have ever been around. Just his medication management alone would have put most parents in a tailspin.

His mom is a great gal. She is solid and has the gift of perspective not everyone has. There is sadness, not in her eyes, but just behind them. I wonder if it's really there or if I am just imagining it? She is not seemingly sad for herself or her situation, she is hurting like many of us do, when we worry about what things in life our children might struggle with, what things they might never enjoy.

Yet, this favorite of mine got out, enjoyed us, as we enjoyed him, and was always a standout at any gathering we had. He is the type of individual who, if you are lucky enough to just be around, makes you a better person.

It was also an environment where we could laugh about things that other people might consider 'cruel'. When you are with parent's that understand the challenges, you are also with people who accept your 'jokes' as comic relief. It's not that we were making fun of our own kids literally…it's that you can have fun with acknowledging the funny side of how things roll out sometimes.

If however, I did happen upon a day where I was venturing towards my pity-pot, it was extraordinarily easy to reflect upon these real live people in my life. People who represented a place I would not want to be.

     Combining what I saw in the newspaper every day, and in my real life relationships, I eliminated a trip to the pity-pot most of the time.

Suggestion

When you are challenged, remind yourself of the troubles in the world around you, and your troubles will seem small.

Chapter 11

Those 'Other' Days…..

Having the ability to stay off the pity-pot "most" days, is another way of saying, there would be those "other" days. I might be coming off a 60 hour work week. The car battery died, the water heater leaked, an unexpected bill from the IRS, or all of the above.

For those 'other days', those days when something hard or emotional comes up and I couldn't talk myself out of my emotions by using a newspaper story, or a real life relationship, I had to allow myself that trip to the pity-pot . And just as importantly, not feel guilty about it.

The funny part is, on those days, it never seemed to be a big event. It never seemed to be my son having an injury on the playground. It wasn't those fearful several moments when he did not come out of school right on-time. It wasn't a teacher sharing an emotional event about my son that would break my heart. It was often something small and inconsequential that would set things off.

I remember one particular evening, nothing earth shattering happened, just a long day at work, picking up my son, preparing dinner, staging homework...etc.

As I flipped on the light and proceeded down the hallway towards my bedroom I encountered what I believed to be a small piece of black lint, sitting there on my very white carpet.

I stopped and looked closer to confirm, it was in fact, a simple piece of black lint. I would normally have just bent down, picked it up, tucking it between my thumb and index finger, tossing it in the closest receptacle. On that day, for some reason, my brain took a sharp left.

When I looked down at that tiny piece of black fuzz all I could think was that if 'I' didn't bend down and pick it up, no one else would. I convinced myself, in what was likely a brain microsecond, that the whole burden of taking care of things fell squarely on my shoulders. If I didn't pick up that 'tiny' black fuzz, no one would come behind me to do it. That 'tiny' black fuzz could grow, and possibly become, a 'large' black fuzz.

If I left it long enough, it might become the size of the dust bunnies we find when we haven't moved the bed frame for awhile to vacuum. Now, almost hallucinating, I imagined it could possibly grow to the size of an enormous tumbleweed, blocking the hallway altogether. It might ultimately become a huge 'lint monster' that could only be removed if I called in an outside service.

Eventually I came back to my senses. I bent down and picked up that tiny particle. I headed towards the back bathroom to dispose of it properly, by flushing it down the toilet. Any other means would not have assured me, it would not return.

At that moment I began to 'tear up'. I had that heavy feeling right in the area I'm sure is my heart. No matter how much I had that 'inner talk' about "getting a grip", the tears kept coming and seemed impossible to stop.

I really wasn't reacting to that tiny fuzz, and how no one would come behind me to pick it up. I was thinking that if I don't get my son ready for the world, no one else will. I was asking myself, "how will he cope?", "how will he get on", "what more should I be doing"?

Clearly, for whatever reason, I was feeling overwhelmed. The newspaper stories weren't enough. Thinking about my partners in parenting, was not enough. At times like these, there was nothing that could keep me grounded.

On those sorts of days, I would allow myself a few moments, maybe more, to retreat to the back room and sit on my pity-pot throne. Picturing an imaginary crown on my head and an imaginary staff in my hand, I could have a nice cry, and be the queen of the pity-pot for a time.

According to research, crying actually has health benefits. Anyone who has had a nice hard cry can confirm the relaxed state it puts you in. Crying, as a result of emotional stress, apparently creates salty tears. Tears which not only contain salt, but also contain stress hormones. Crying results in the release of these stress hormones from the body. So, regardless of what was going on in the world, or in my own backyard, it was OK to cry. It was actually healthy.

As I returned to reality, I always felt better. I was again able to use the diversions of a newspaper story, or thoughts of folks I knew, to ground me. However, I did have to work on not allowing myself to feel guilty if I had to take that occasional trip to the pity-pot.

Suggestion

When all else fails, allow yourself to throw a Pity-Party, have a good cry, and never ever feel guilty about it.

Chapter 12

"ALL ABOARD "

    I can't quite put my finger on the exact time, but somewhere between middle school and high school things were changing at almost lightning speed. He was communicating more. He was creating CD's which combined graphics and music. He continued to read lots of books on trains, but the types of books expanded to include stories being written by railroaders.

    To my knowledge, he had no formal training in many of these things. They were things he was thinking about and creating on his own. Things he was gleaning from time spent on the computer perhaps. Oh gee…just like a typical teenager discovering their own thoughts and feelings and applying them to their life. A life, that didn't always include a parent.

My son was maturing and was becoming an even more interesting person. I was starting to see many of the things I had put into place, and had 'waited' for, paying off.

We were by no means "out of woods" yet. We were at the station, ready to board the train. There were so many things coming down that track that my focus and my commitment to him remained ferociously intact.

Many amazing things, and many amazing moments came. He would excel in a subject at school, or mention something exceptionally observant or clever. Out of nowhere he was beginning to engage in very typical conversation, even when it wasn't about trains.

Like all parents I was thankful and viewed my son as a precious gift. Now I began to revel in the things that made my son unique. I began to view my parenting in an uncommon situation, as being the recipient of something quite extraordinary.

For all intents and purposes, I began to feel 'lucky'. I couldn't imagine why I would ever want a more typical life. I couldn't picture the boredom of having to roll through a situation without the added value of having to formulate a strategy.

Having to deliberate, or mull over, how I would handle a particular situation, even a simple one, became a welcomed aspect of my life. When things didn't go so well, I had to learn from it. When things went well, there was a sense of pride. If nothing else it sure as hell "kept me on my toes".

That is when I started living a life that took into account, my own advice, in which making my son more 'typical' wasn't the goal. In these early years it was my job to keep him safe, happy, progressing and surviving in the smaller and more controlled world we lived in. It was also my job to anticipate what he would encounter in the future, putting into place habits and routines that I would have to wait and see if they paid off.

Most importantly, I would have to see him as an individual who had exceptional capabilities. I would have to incorporate those capabilities or strengths if you will, into a way of life that would prepare him for independence.

We started at some point to have this little ritual, the kind only families understand, like nicknames. To this day when there's a great little moment, or something new and wonderful surprises me, I ask him, "How did I get so lucky?" He always answers, "Me".

www.ingramcontent.com/pod-product-compliance
Ingram Content Group UK Ltd.
Pitfield, Milton Keynes, MK11 3LW, UK
UKHW022232230426
12048UKWH00016BA/1203